Double Dots

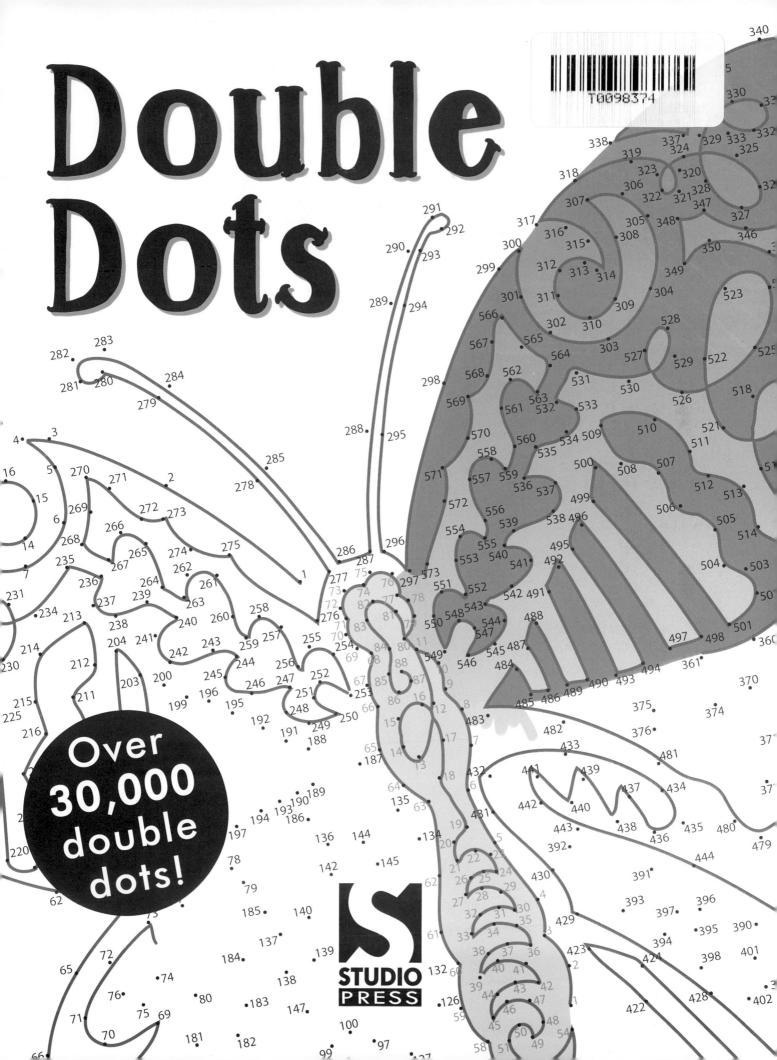

Over 30,000 double dots!

STUDIO PRESS

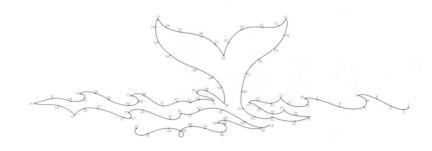

DOUBLE DOTS

HOW TO USE THIS BOOK

Double Dots is a dot-to-dot challenge like no other,
where pictures transform before your eyes!

Each page features double dots; two sets of dots to connect,
revealing a hidden picture for you to colour.

First connect the dots with grey numbers to create the first picture
then transform the image by completing the second set of dots.
Finally add colour to complete your amazing double dot work of art.

There are 60 hidden dot-to-dot pictures for you
to complete and 30,000 double dots to connect.

Discover a caterpillar changing into a butterfly, a tadpole
that becomes a frog, a leaf transforming into a bird,
a duckling that grows into a swan and many more.

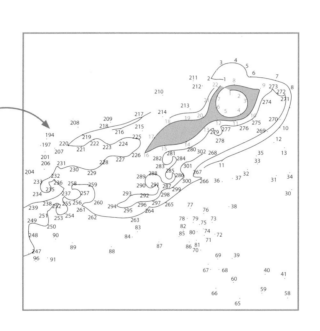

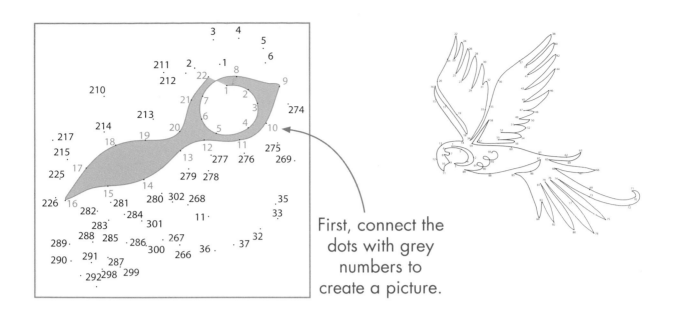

First, connect the dots with grey numbers to create a picture.

Then connect the dots with black numbers to transform your image and reveal the hidden picture.

Finally, colour and complete your double dot art!

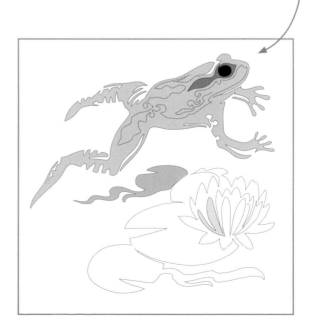

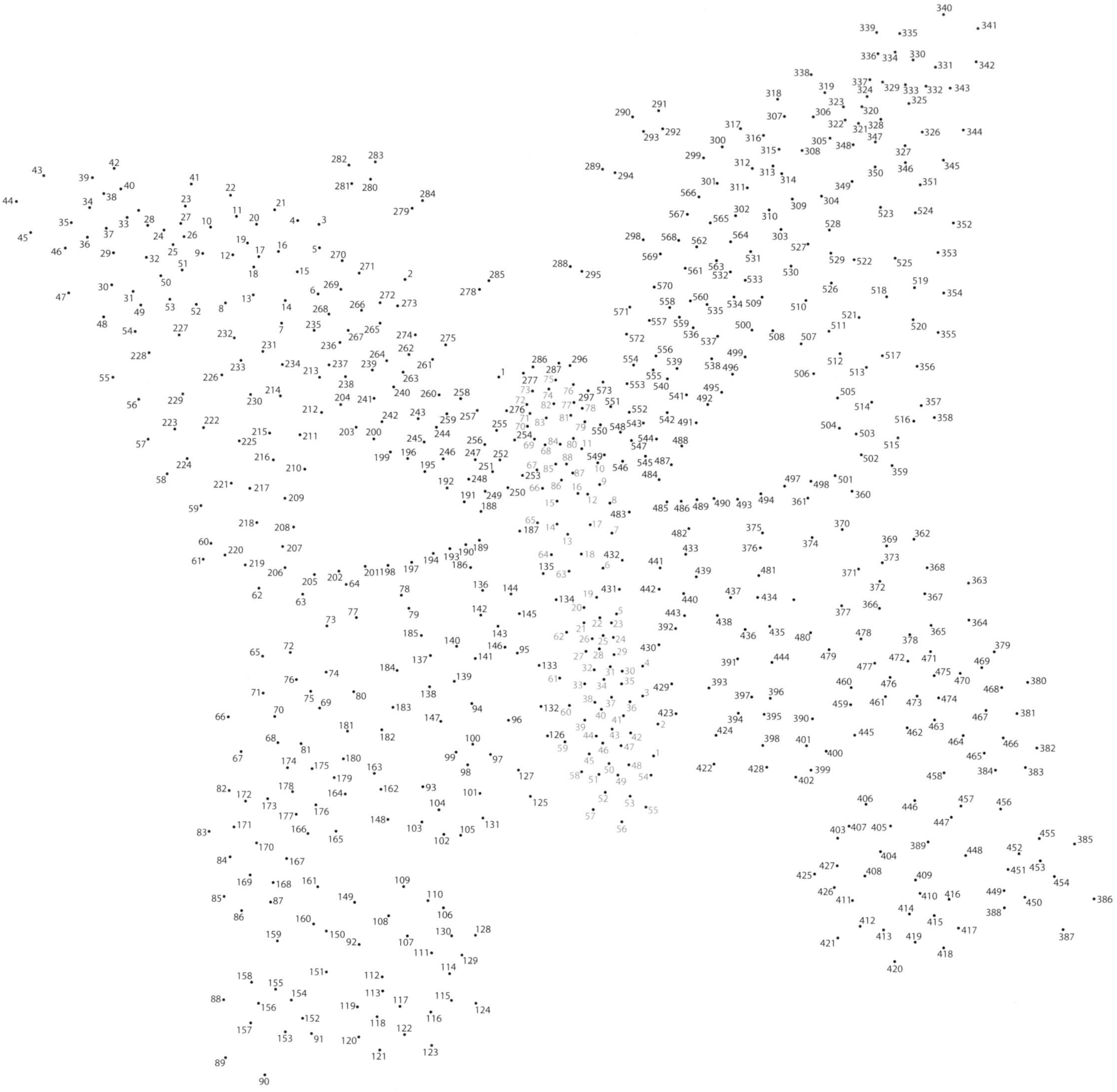

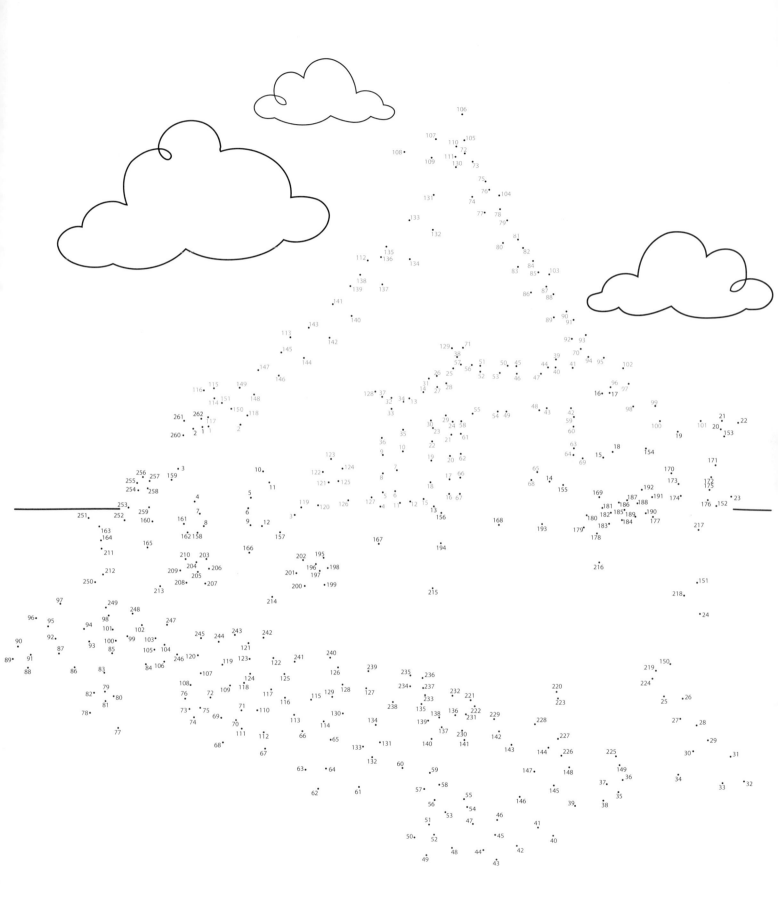

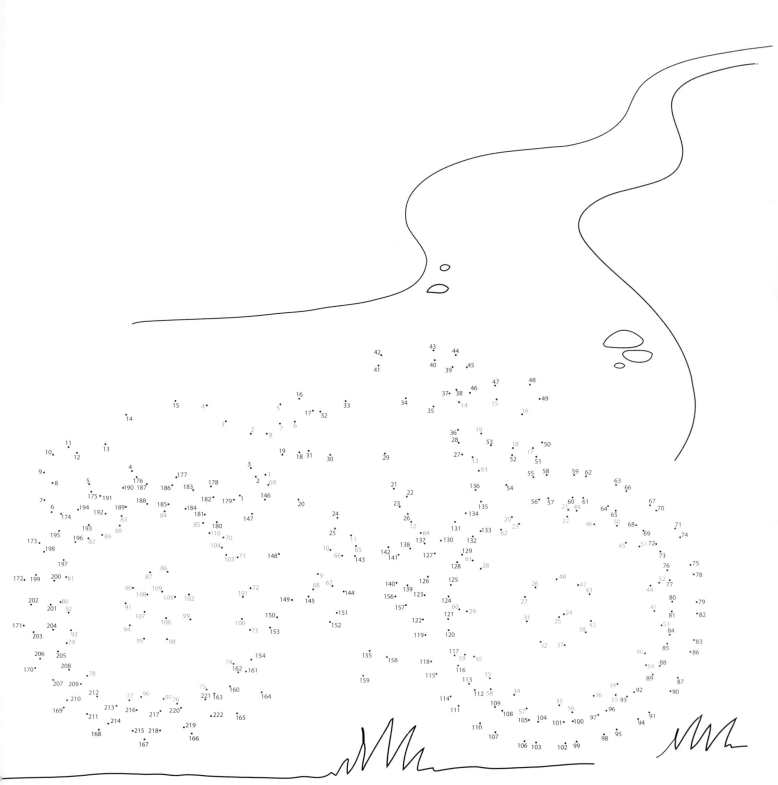

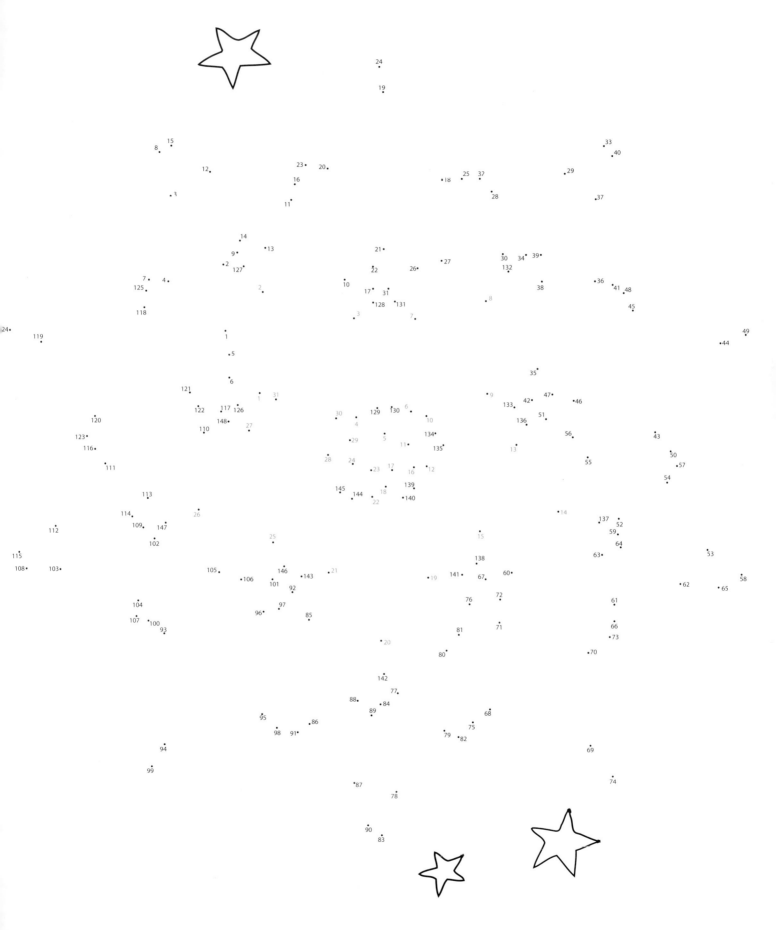

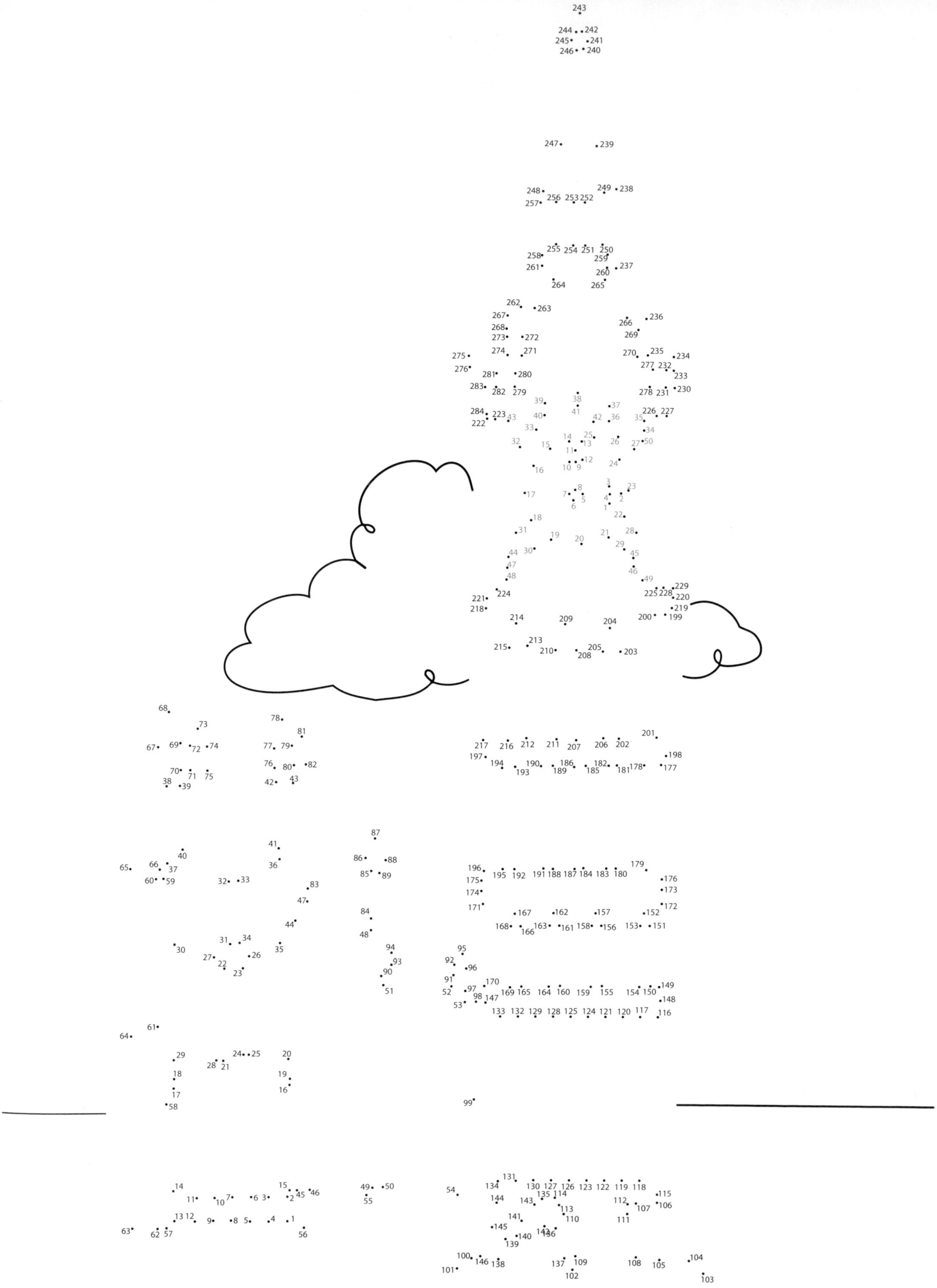

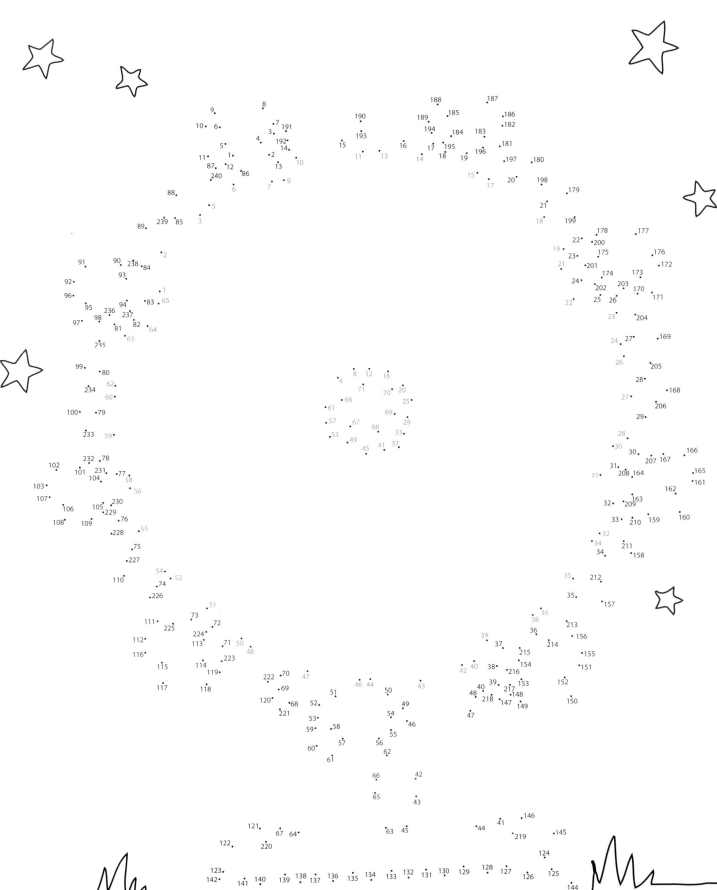

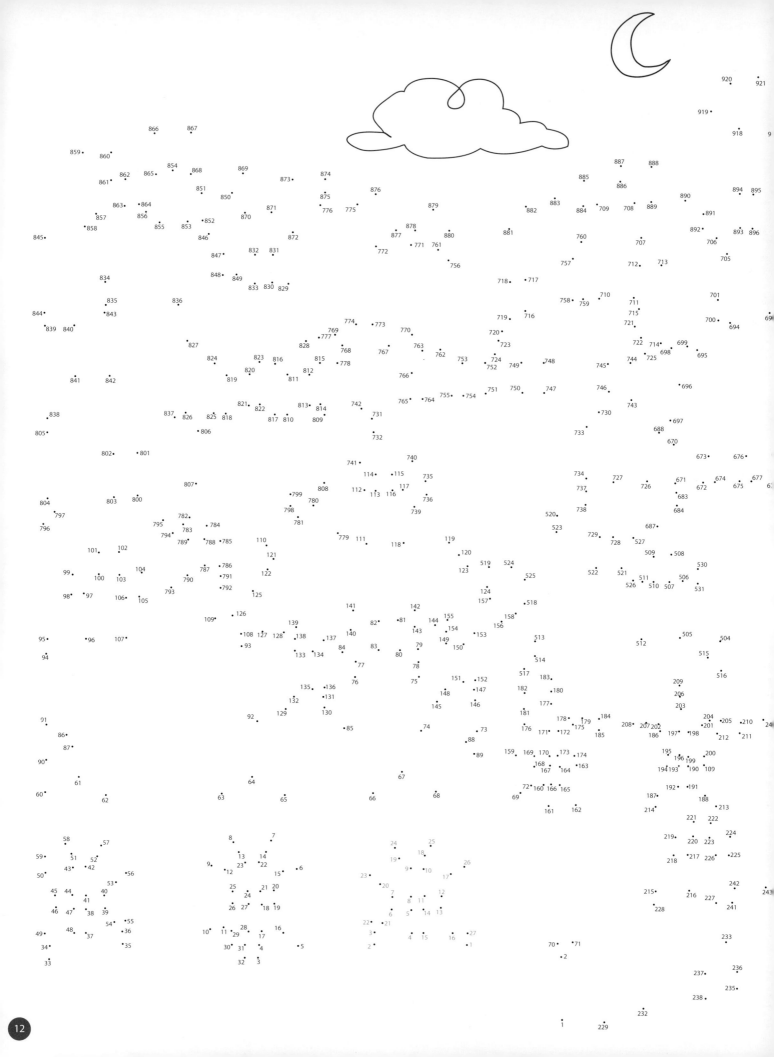

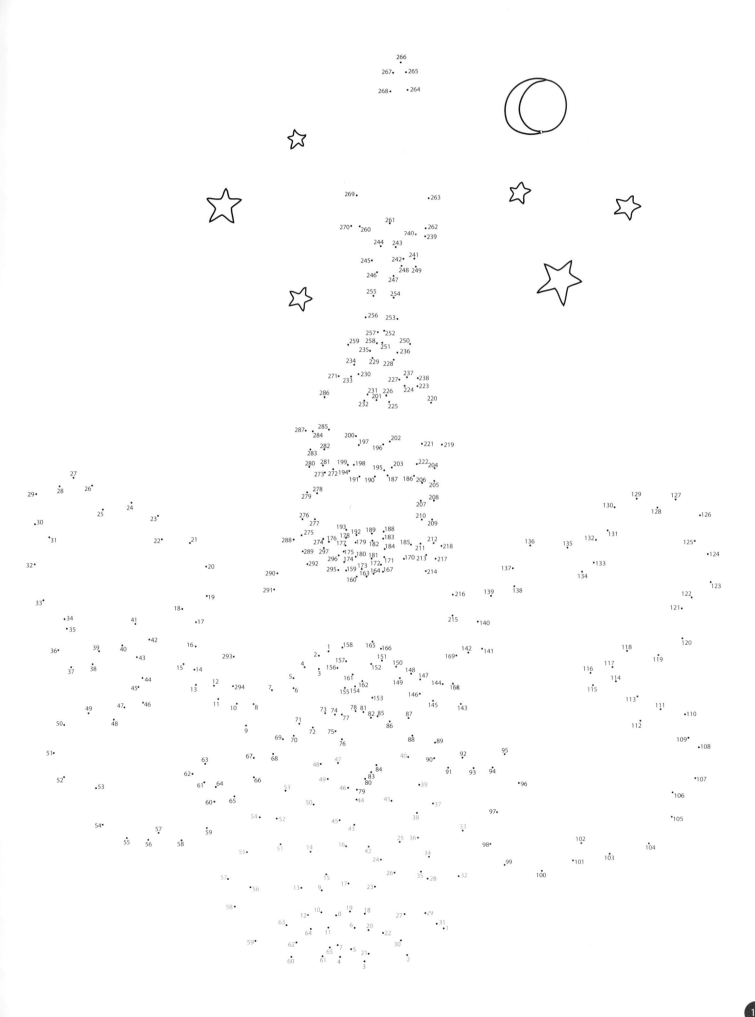

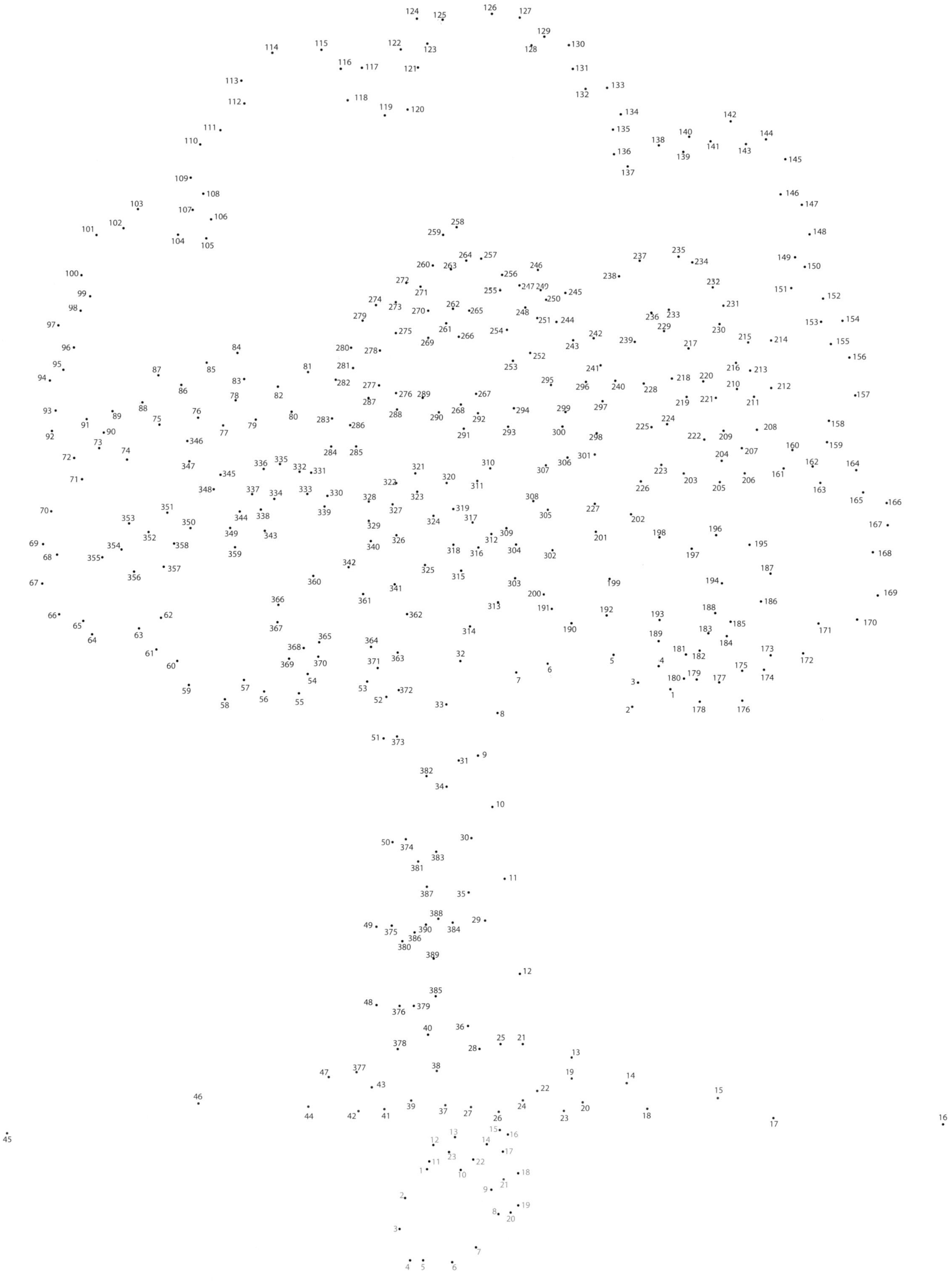

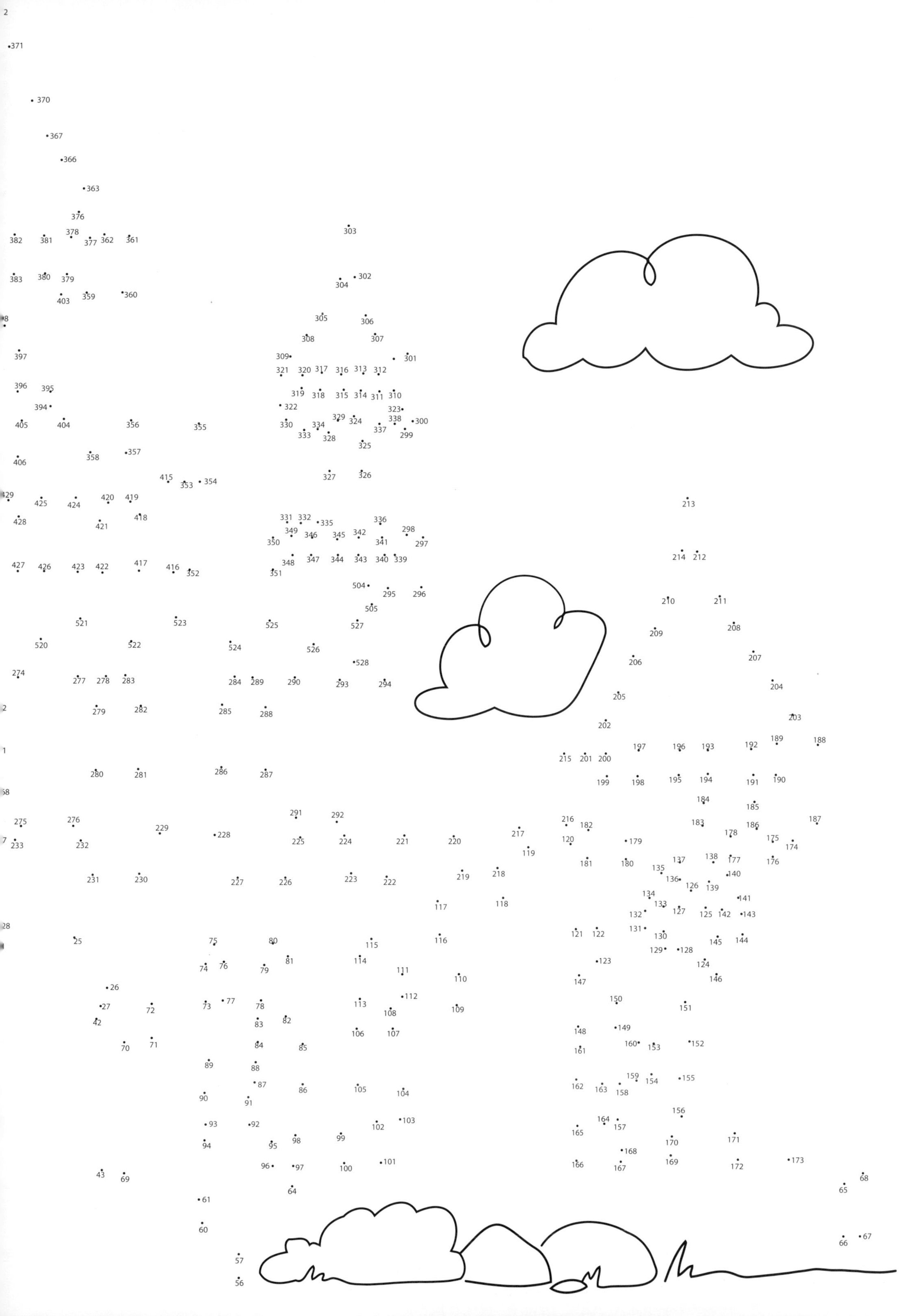

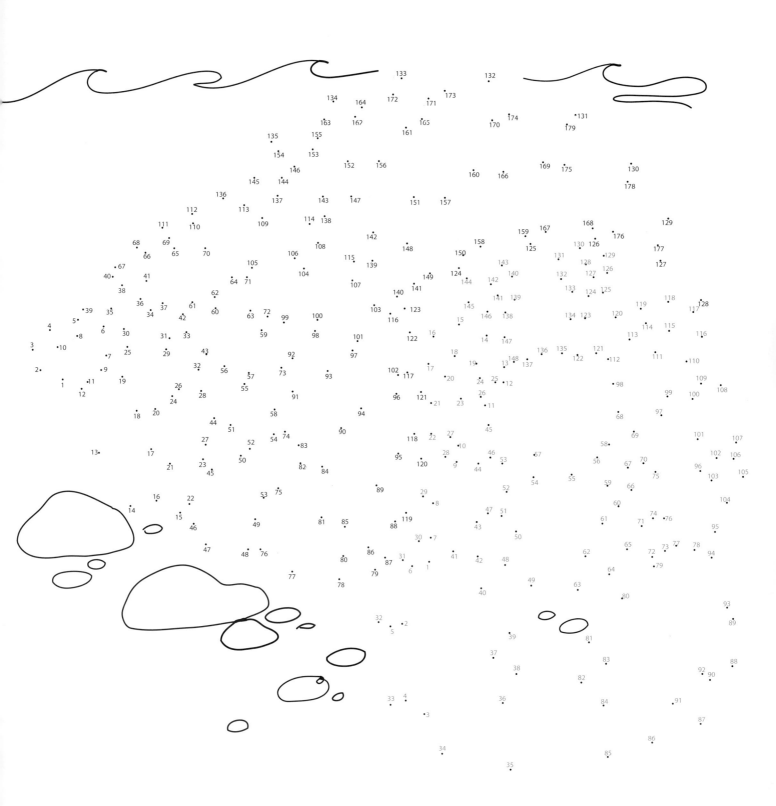

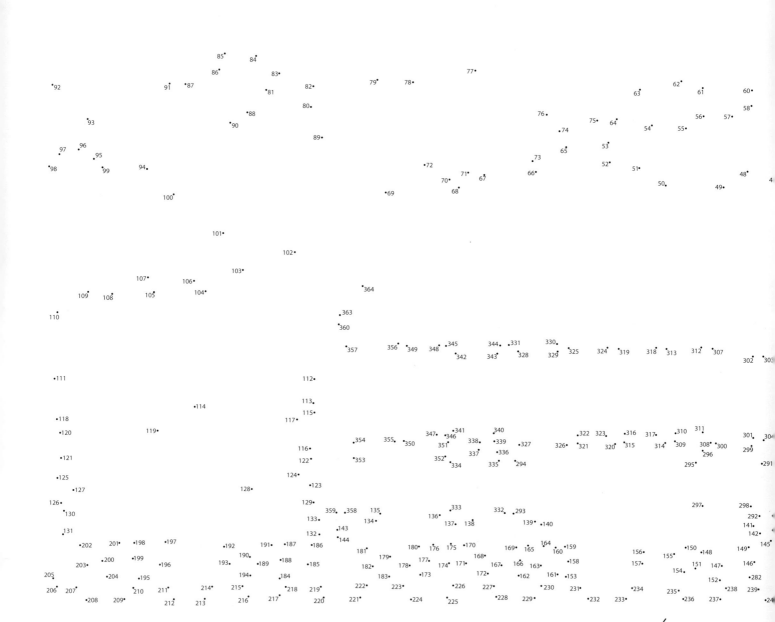

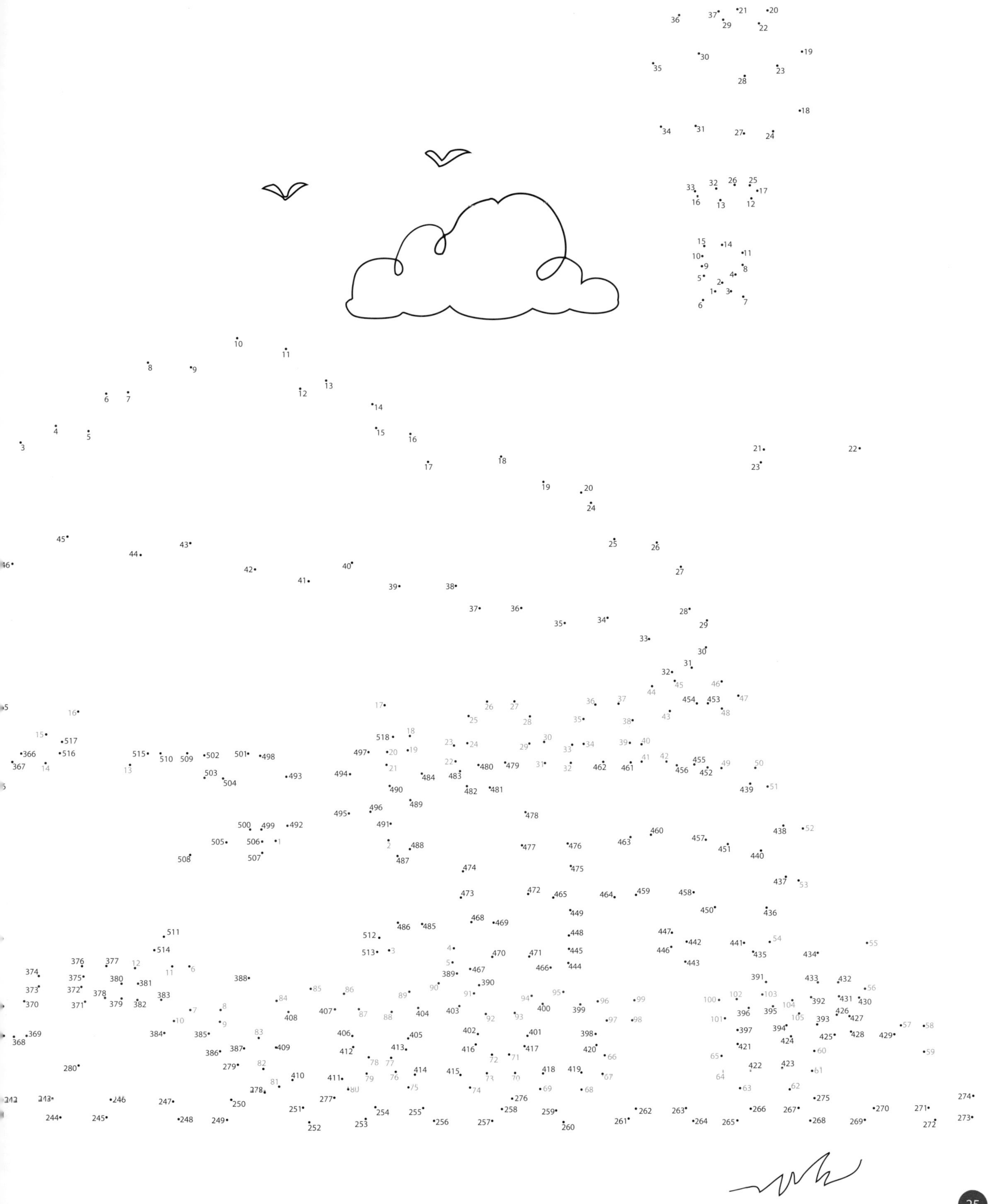

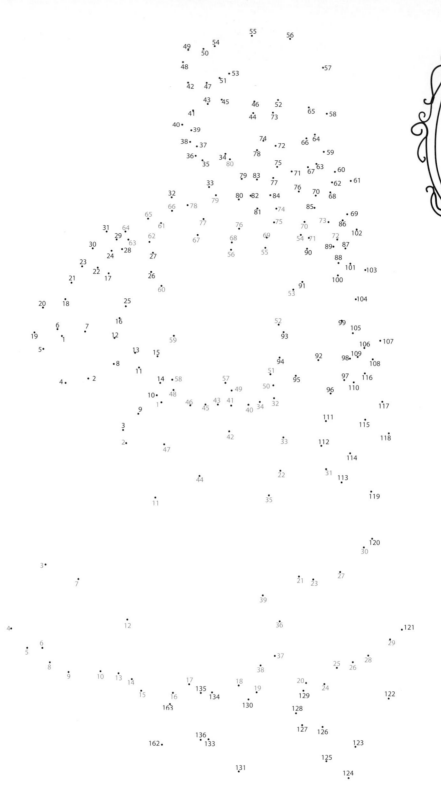

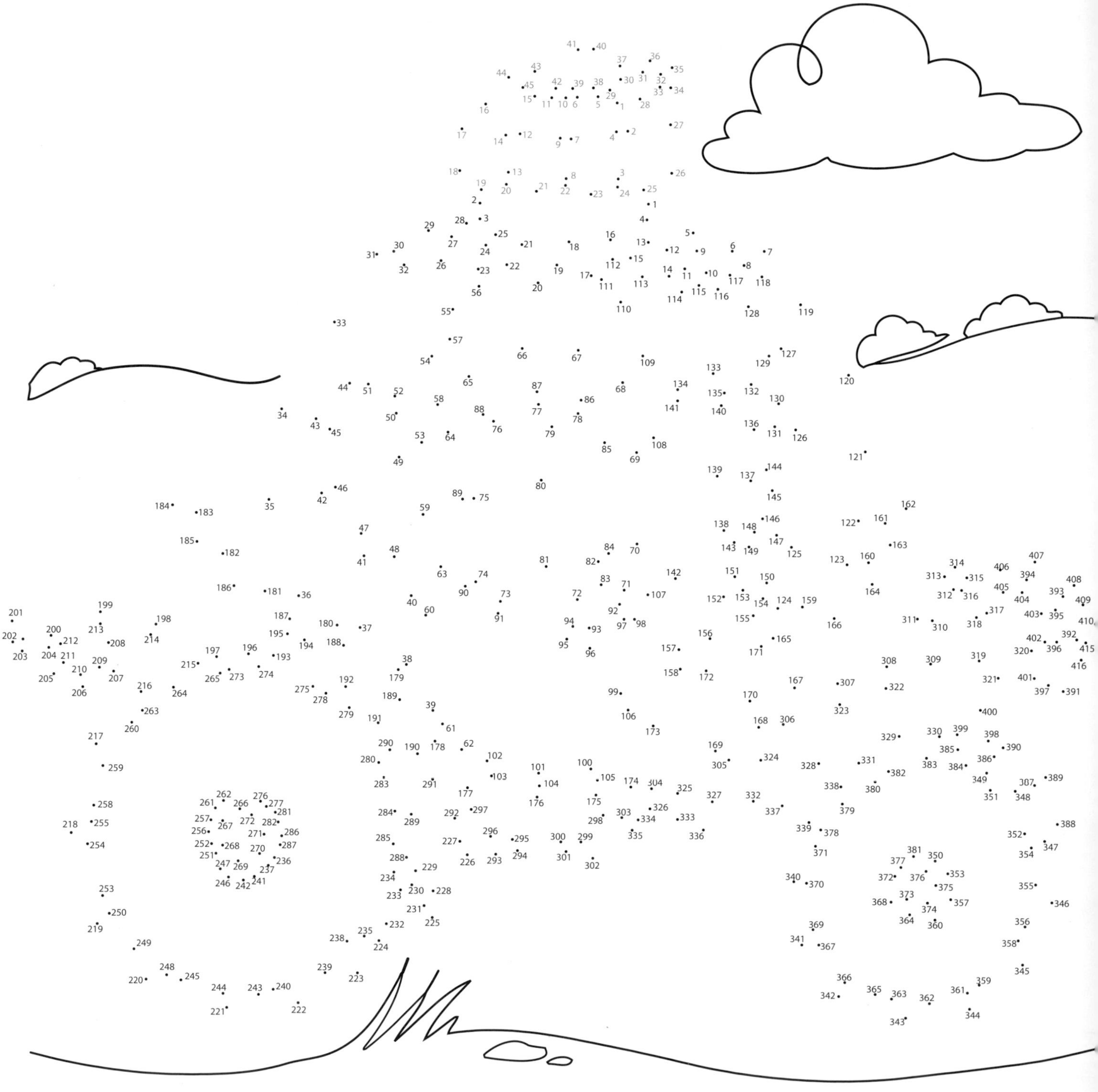

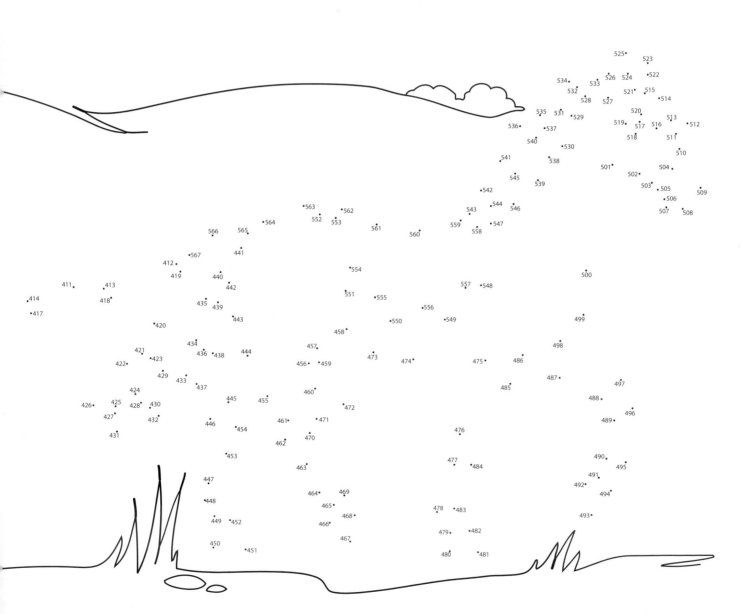

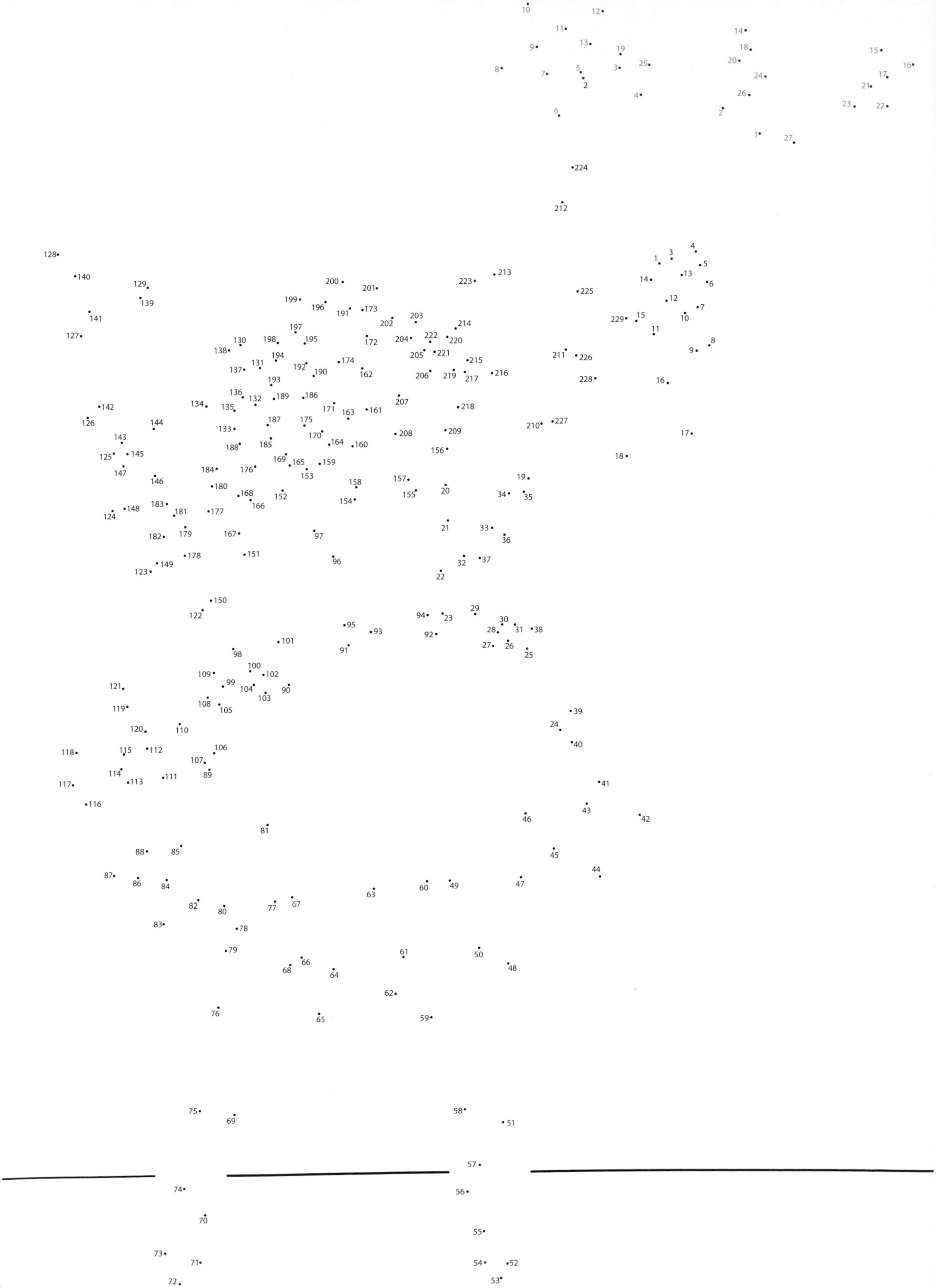

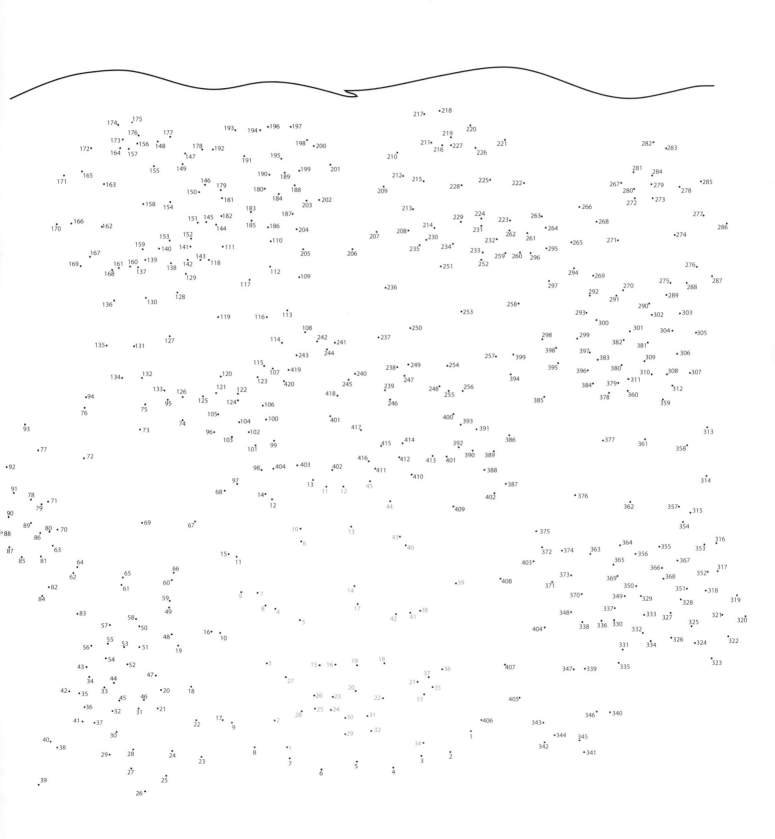

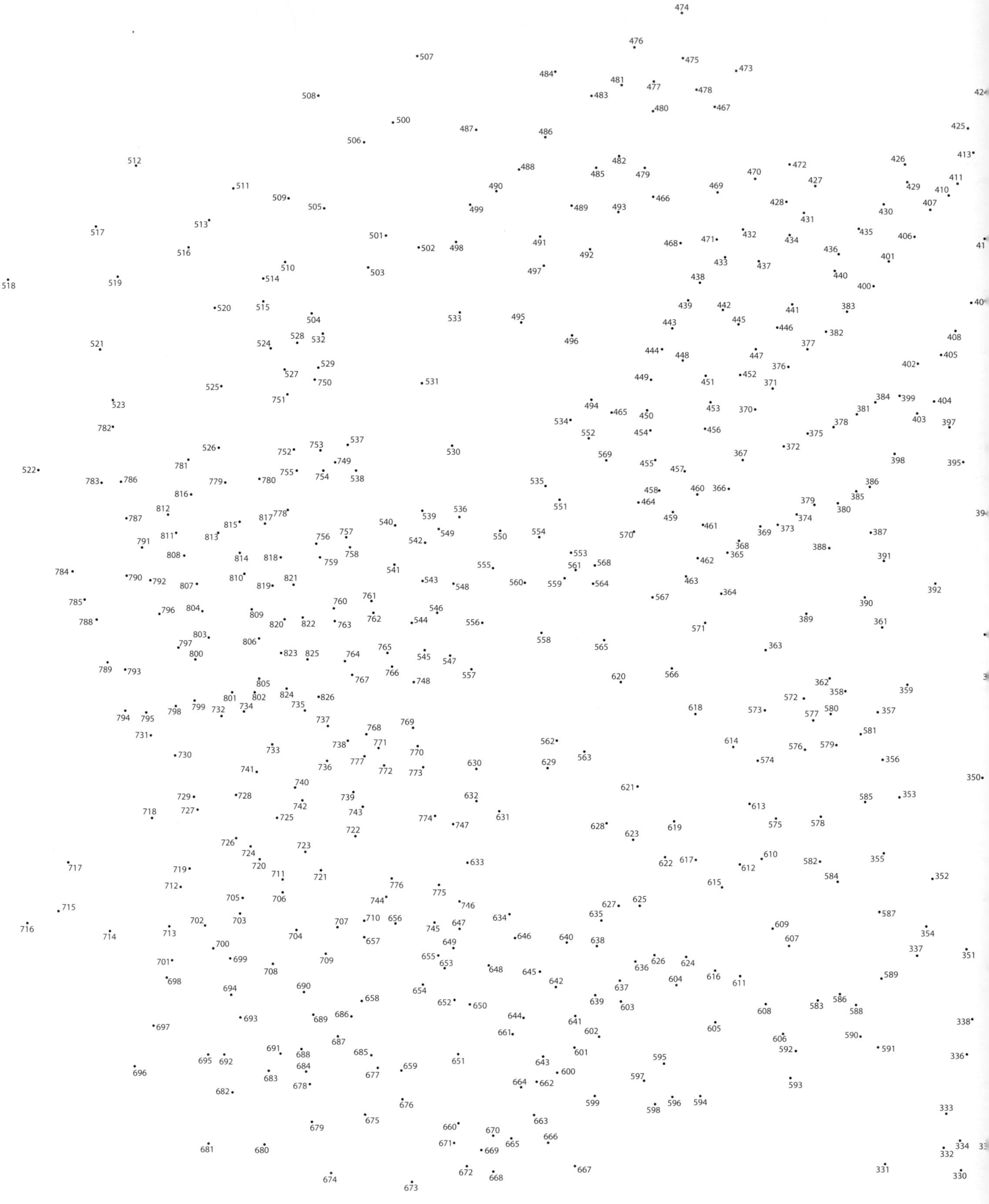

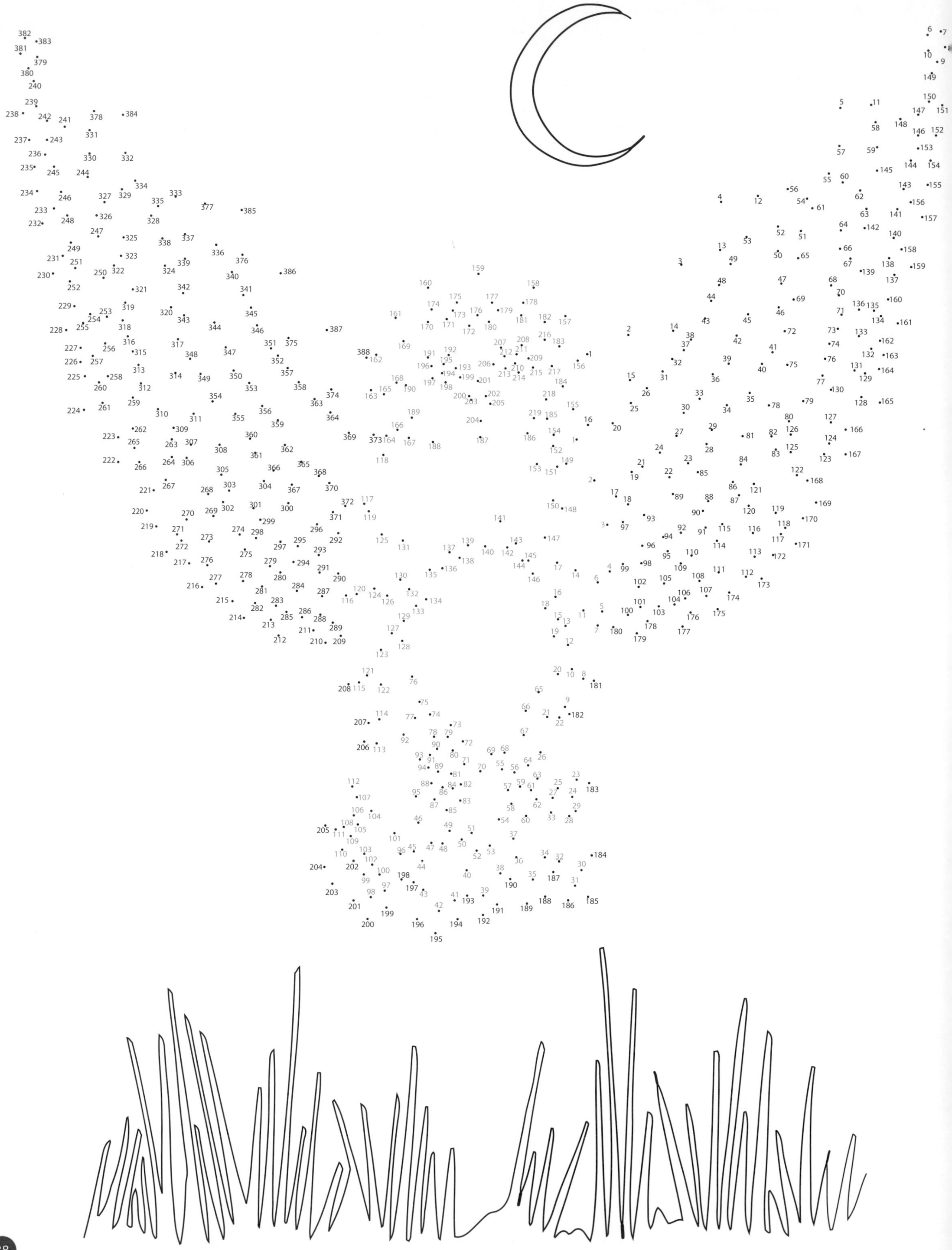

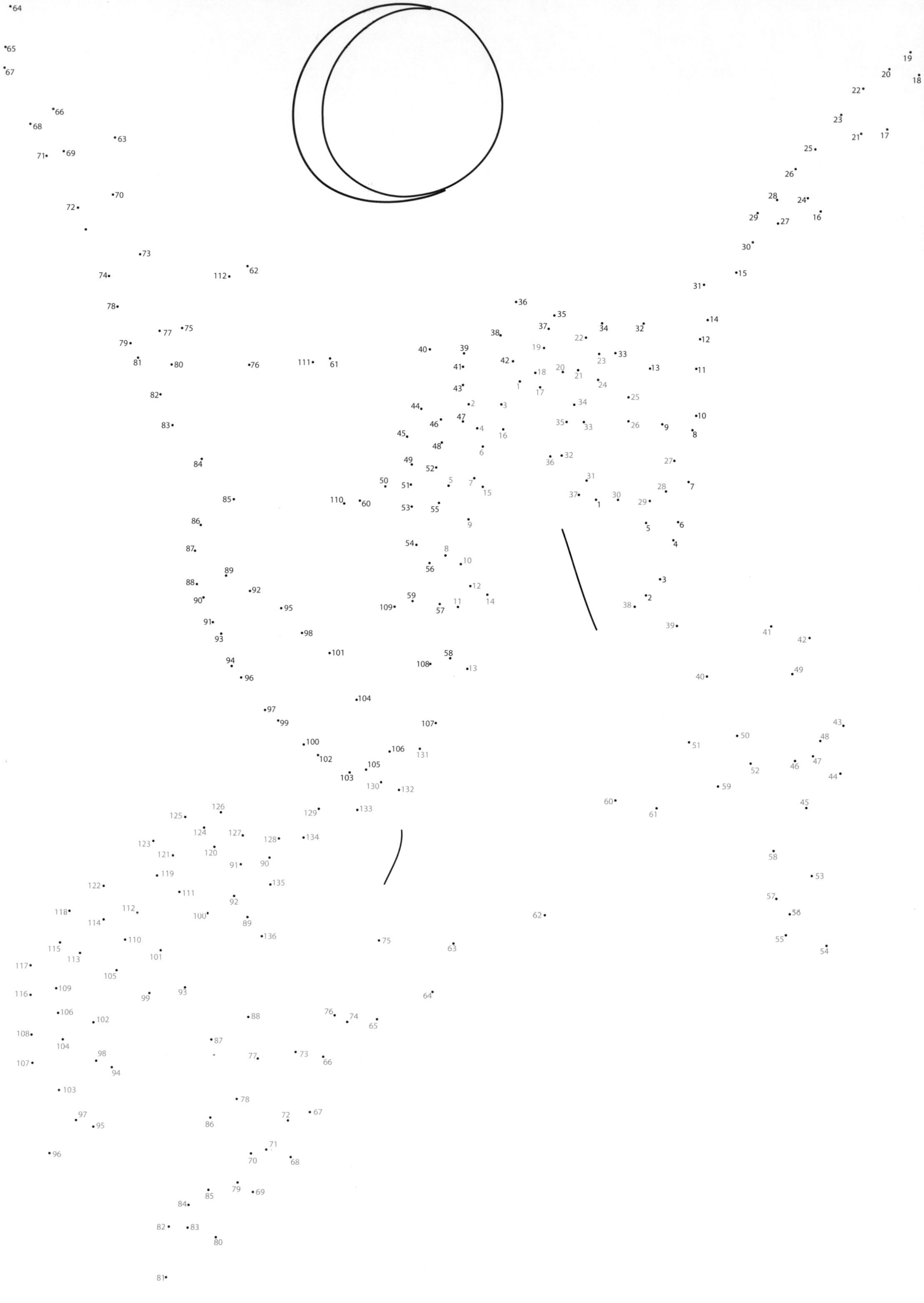

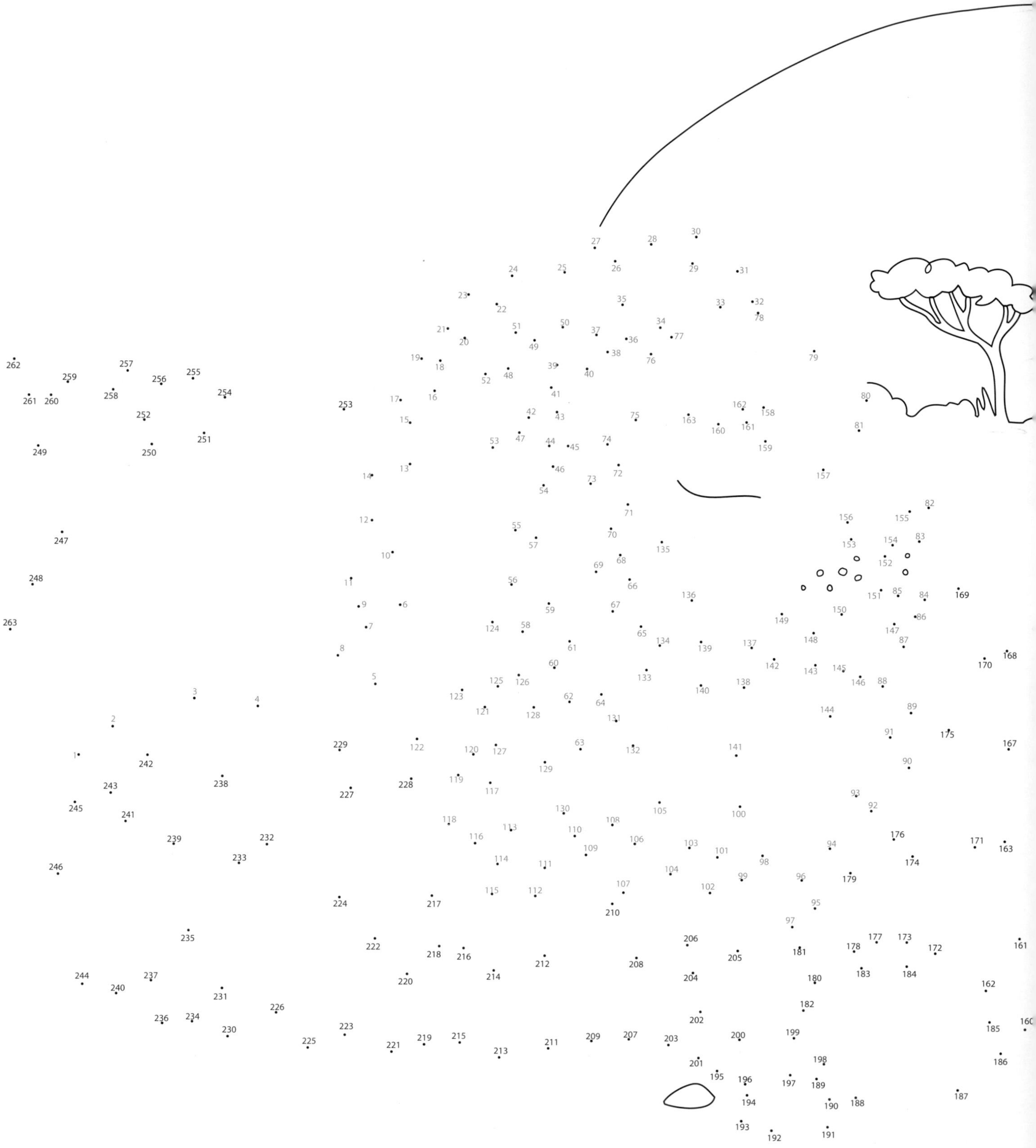

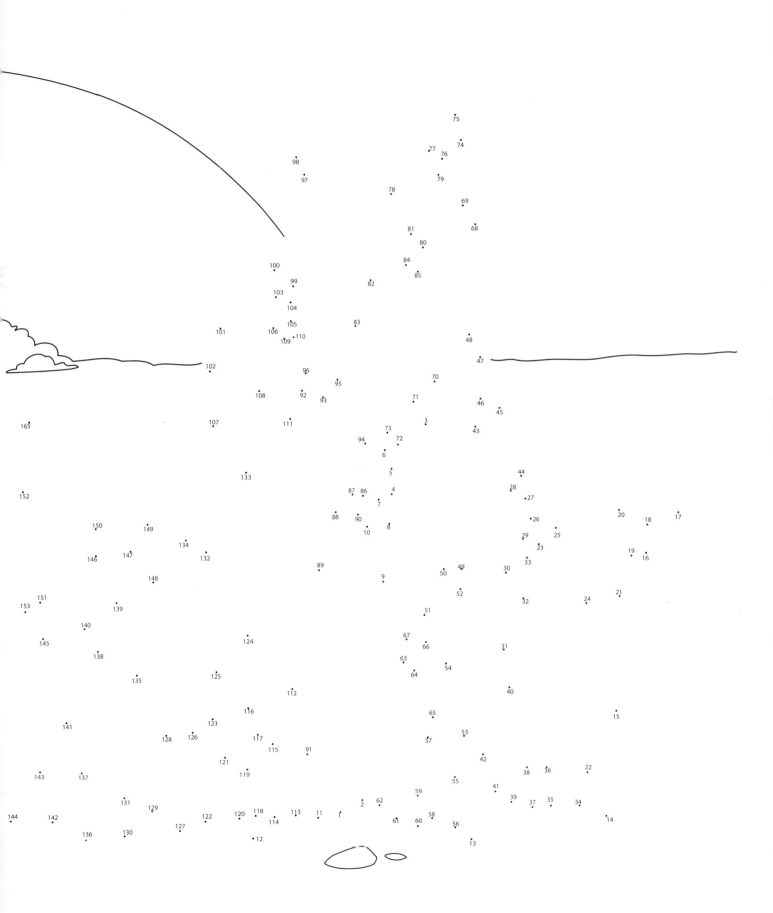

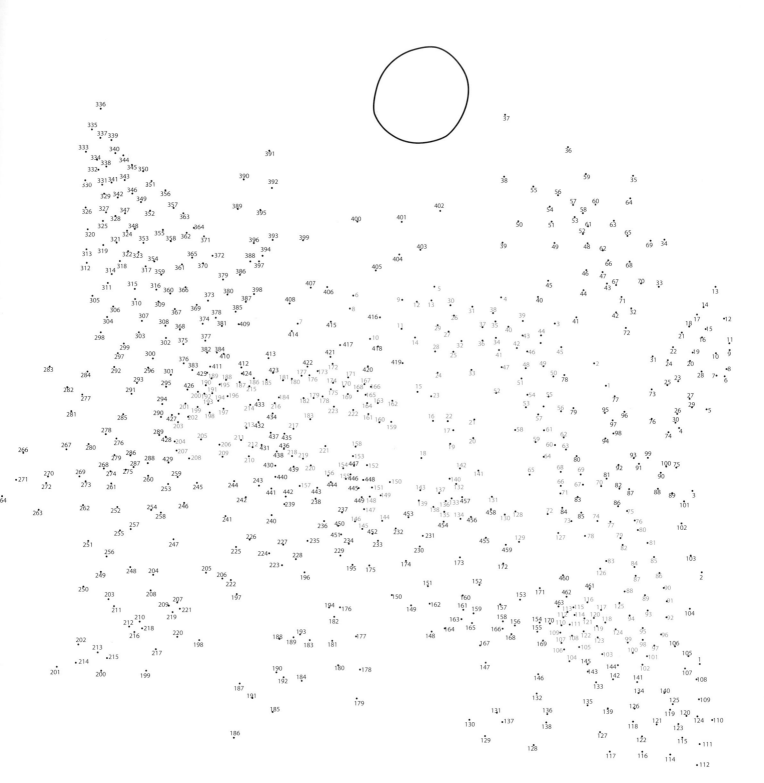

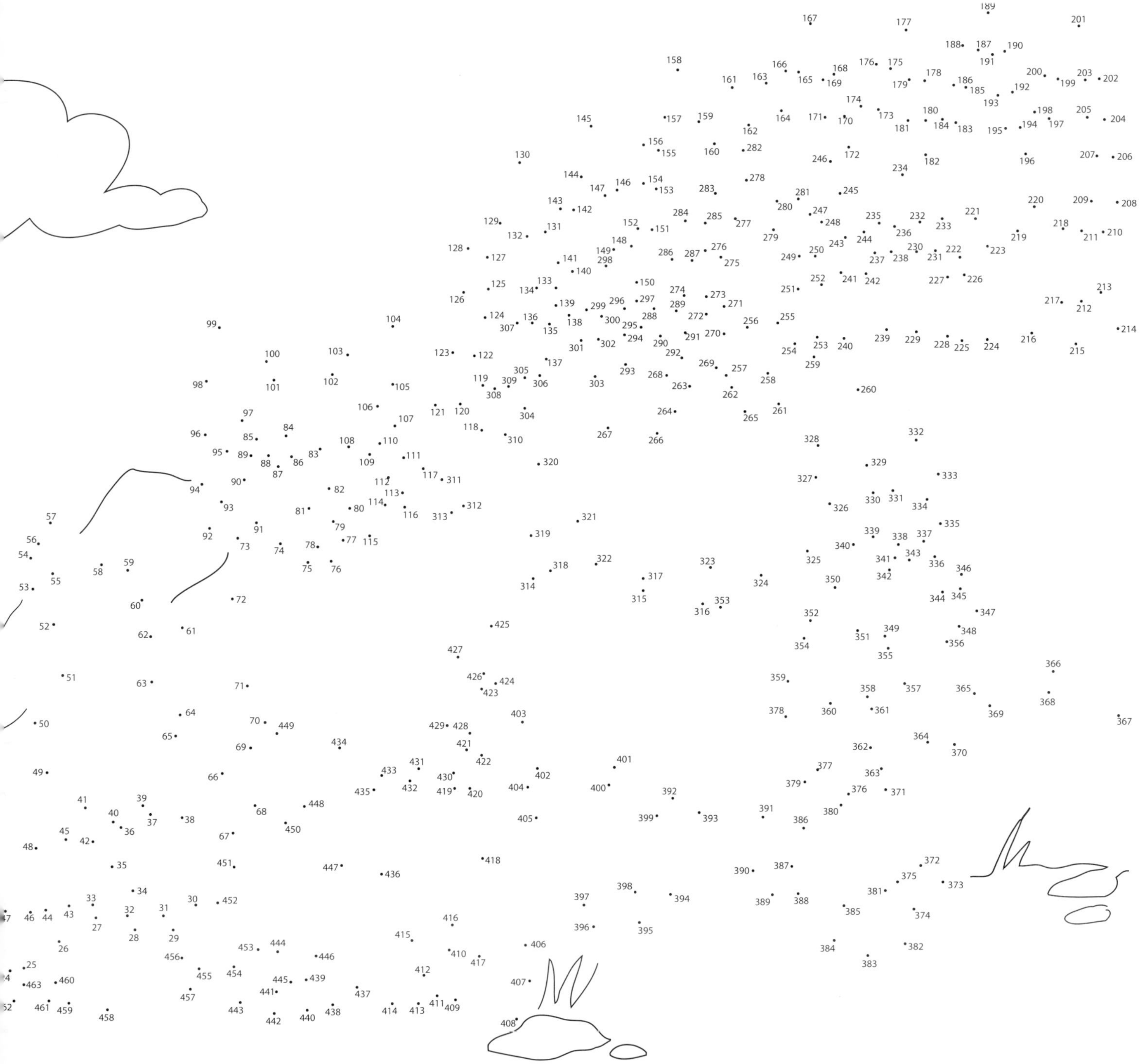

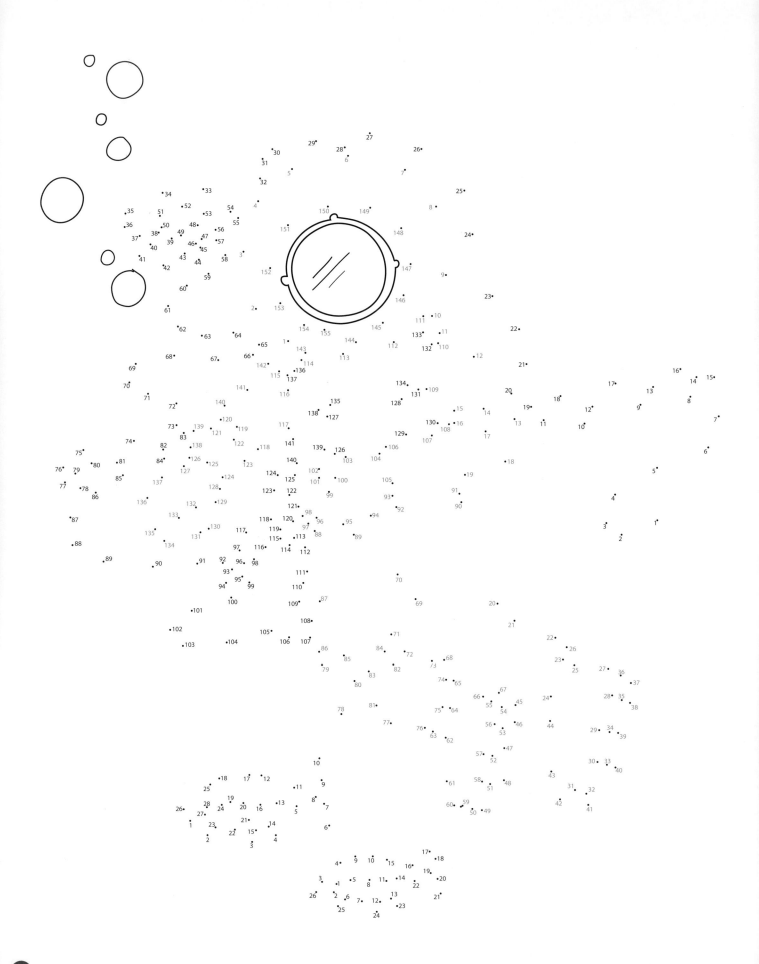

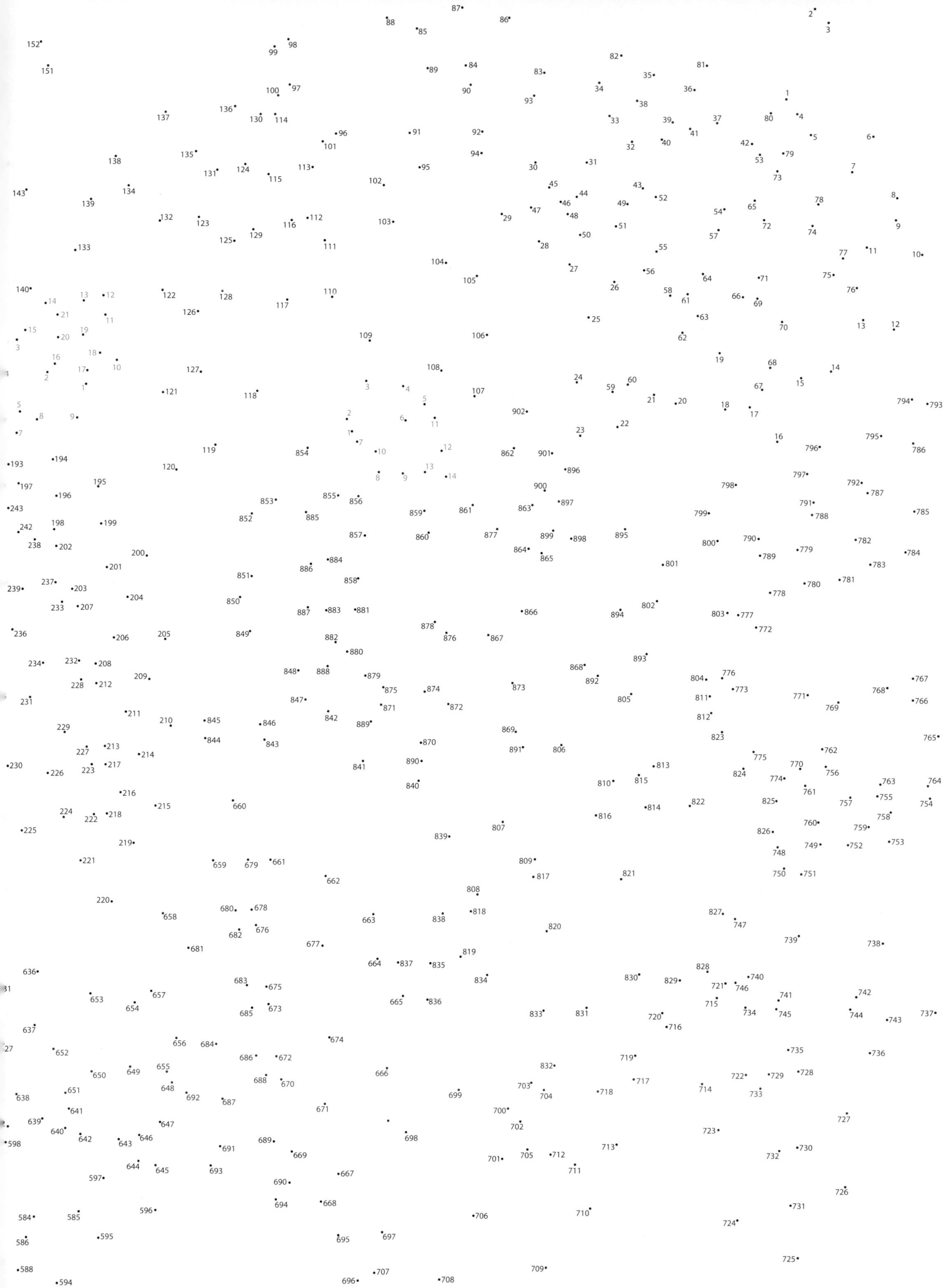

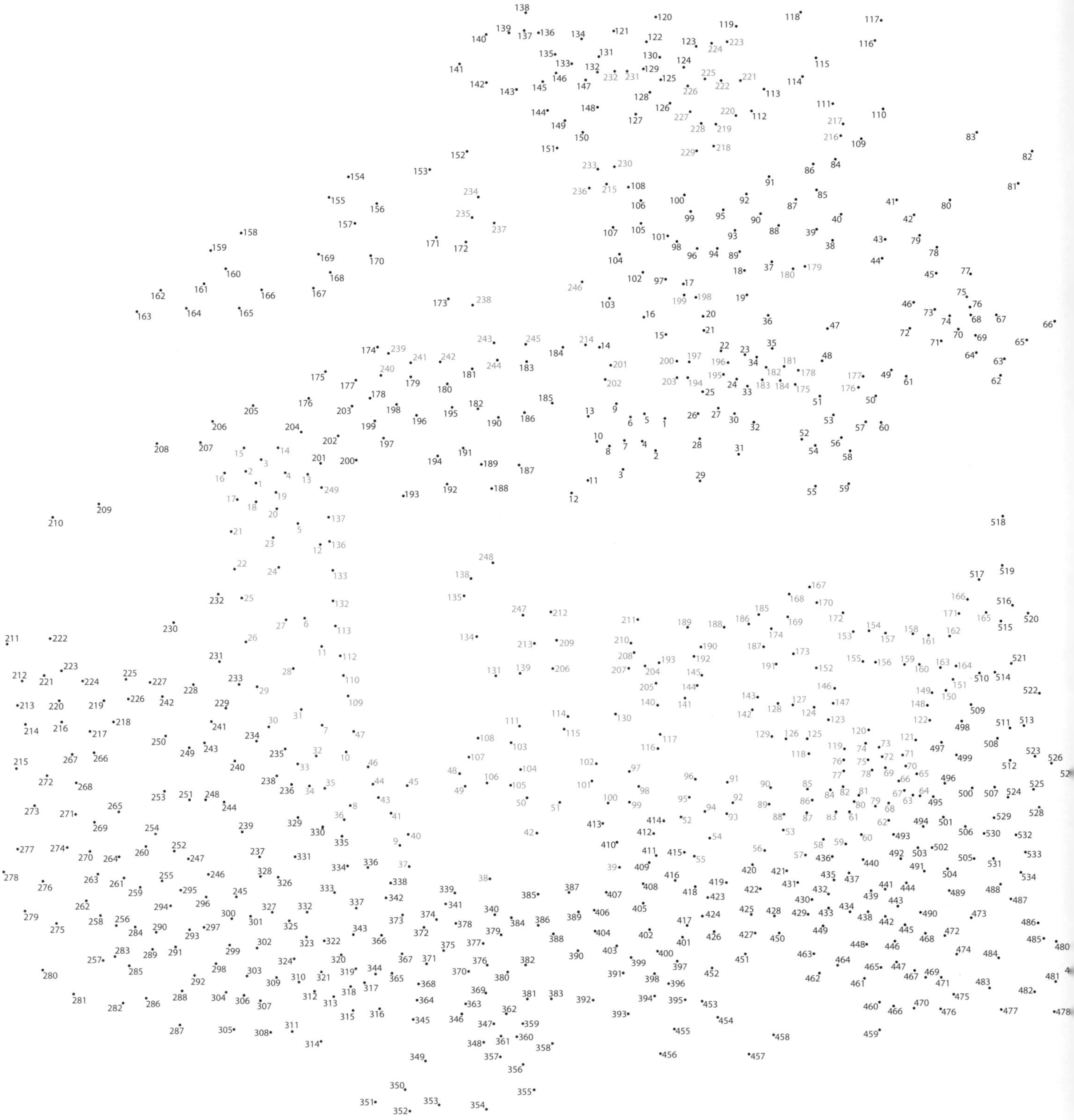

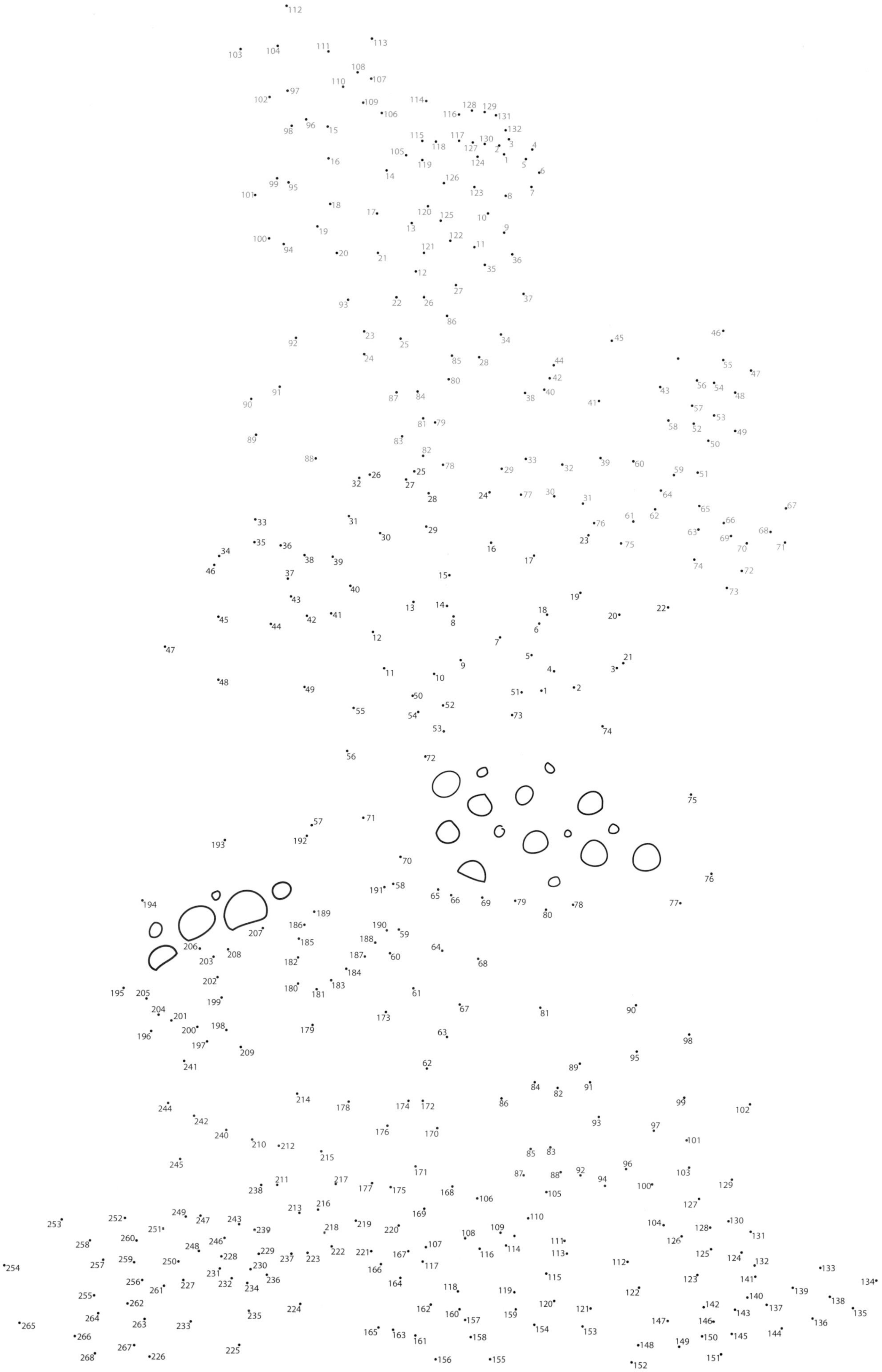

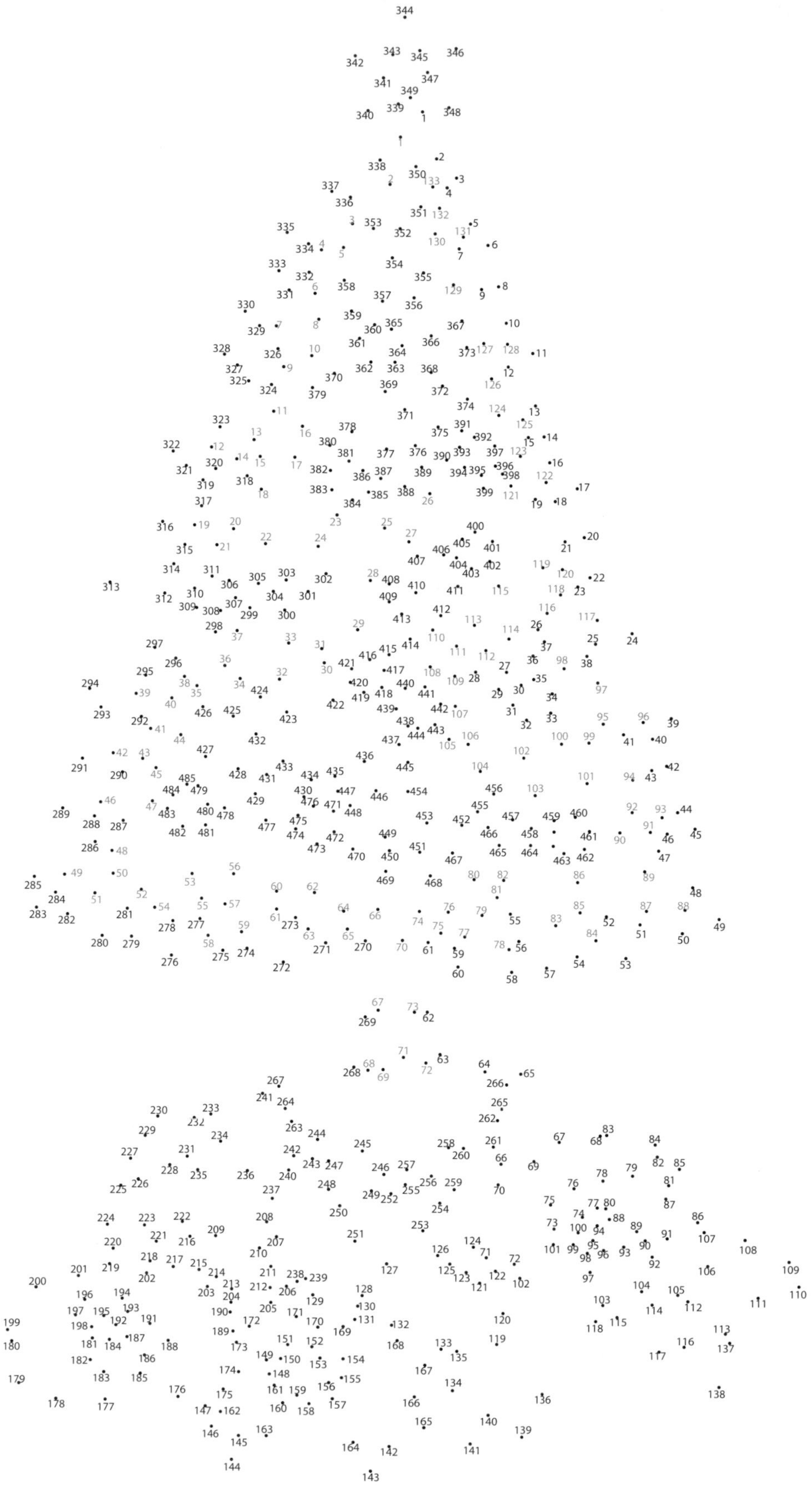

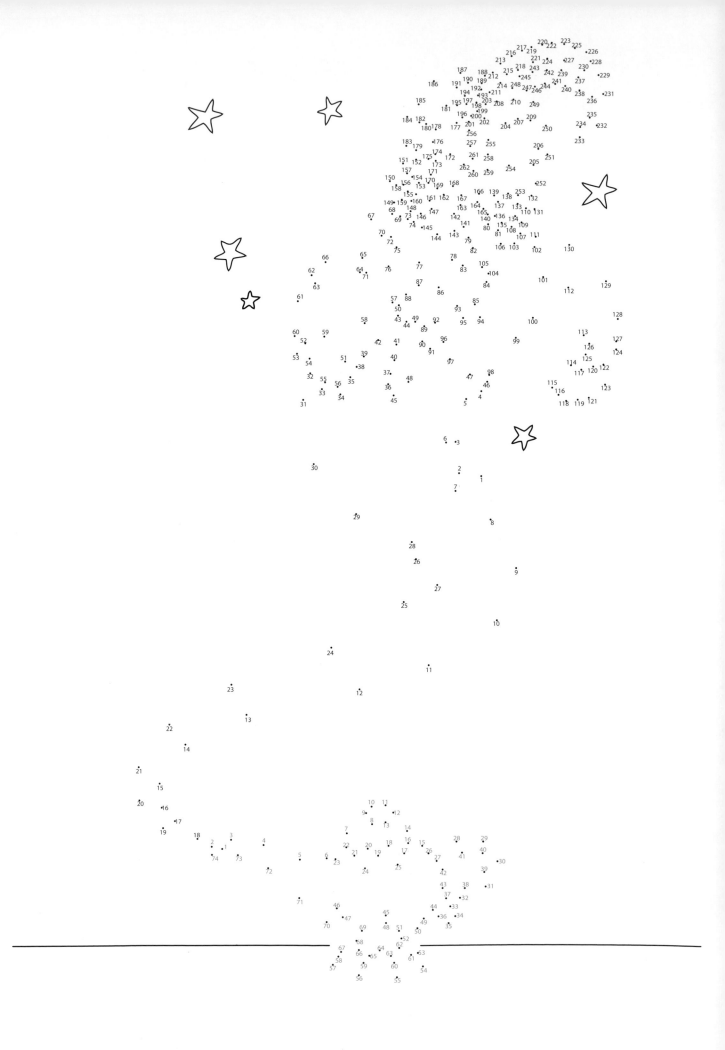

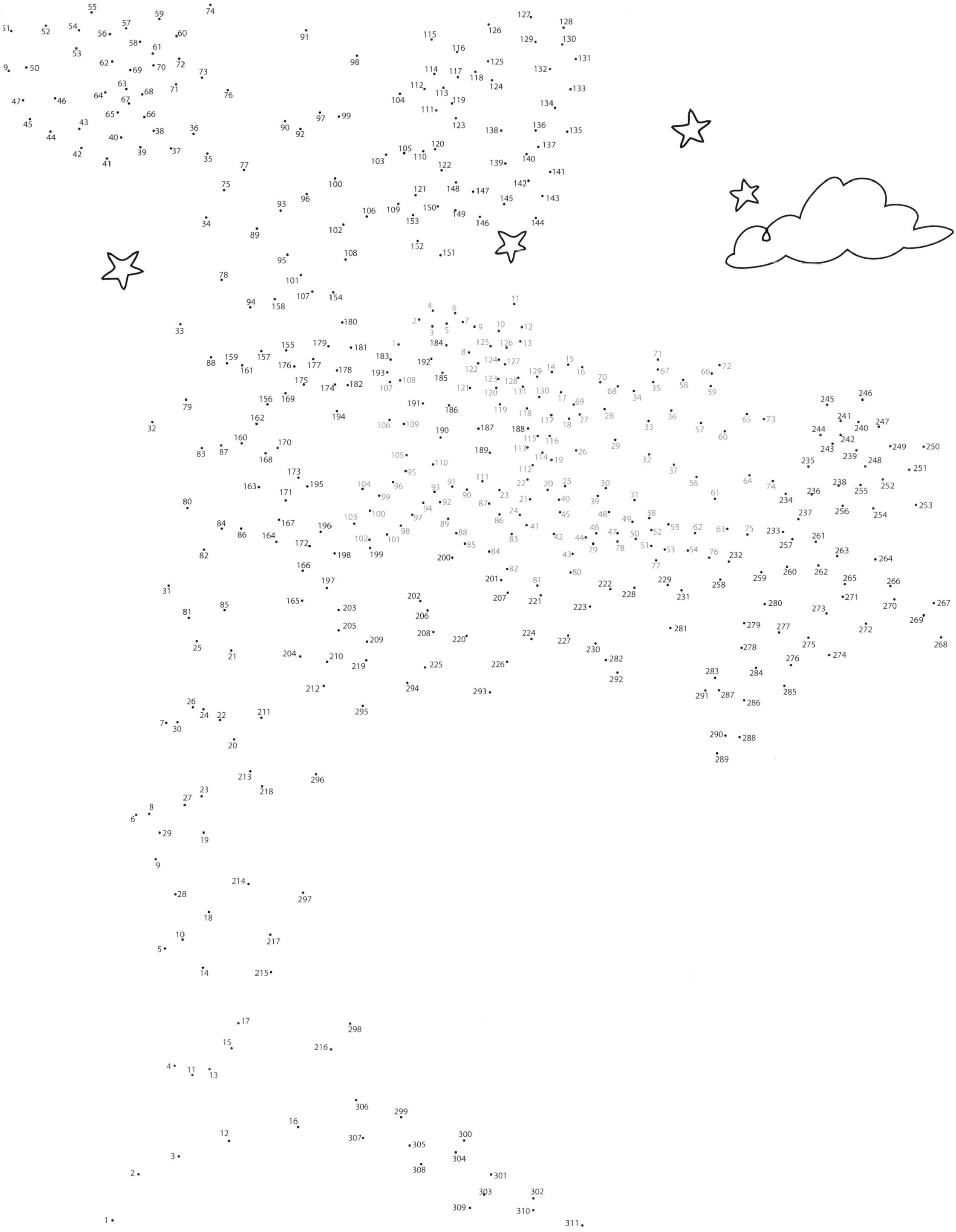

653 • 652   39
656 655
658
659
661   657 651
662 663 654   40
665 664 660
666 667   650
          649
                42
            648
668   647
    644   645   43
        646
    643
                45
669
        47
    642
        641
670   625
    640   62
        639
671   611
        672
      673
601

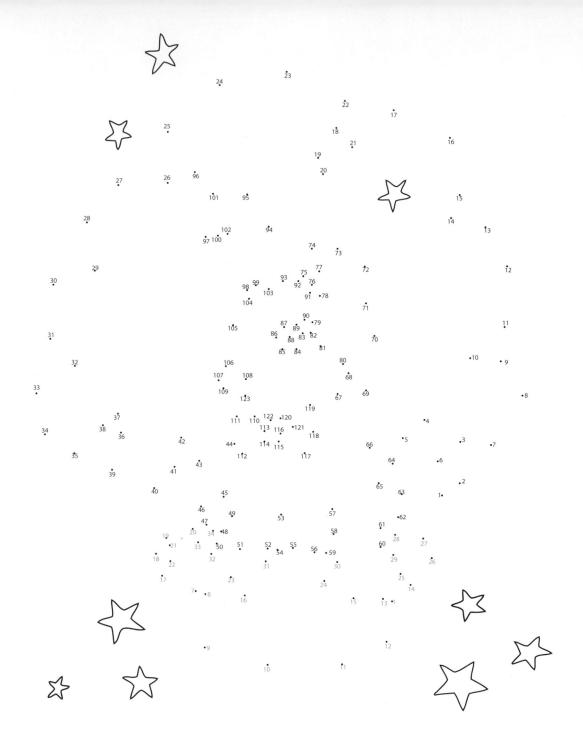
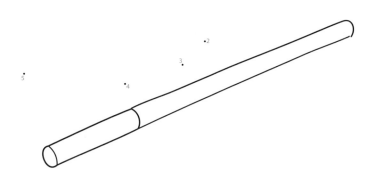

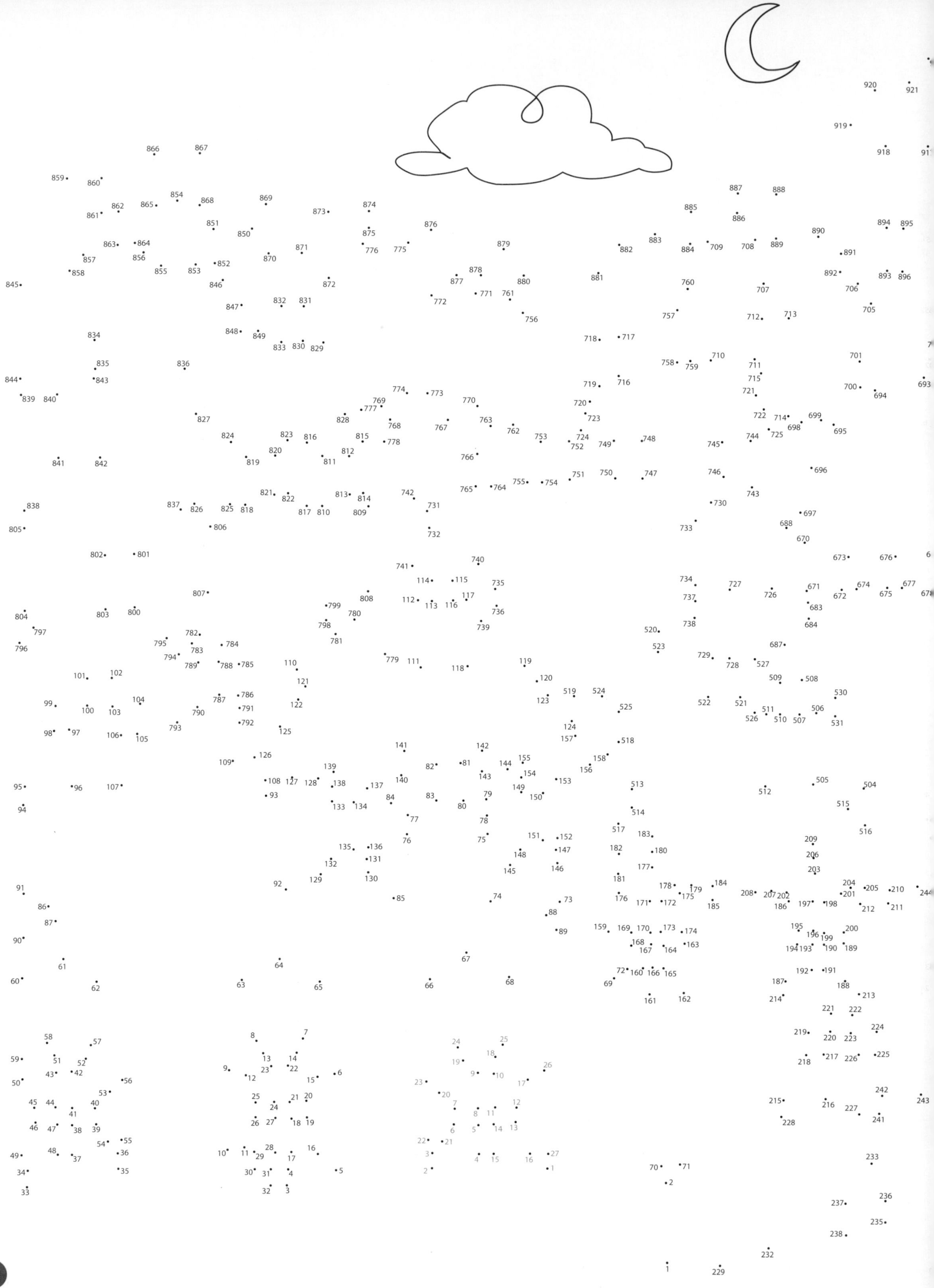

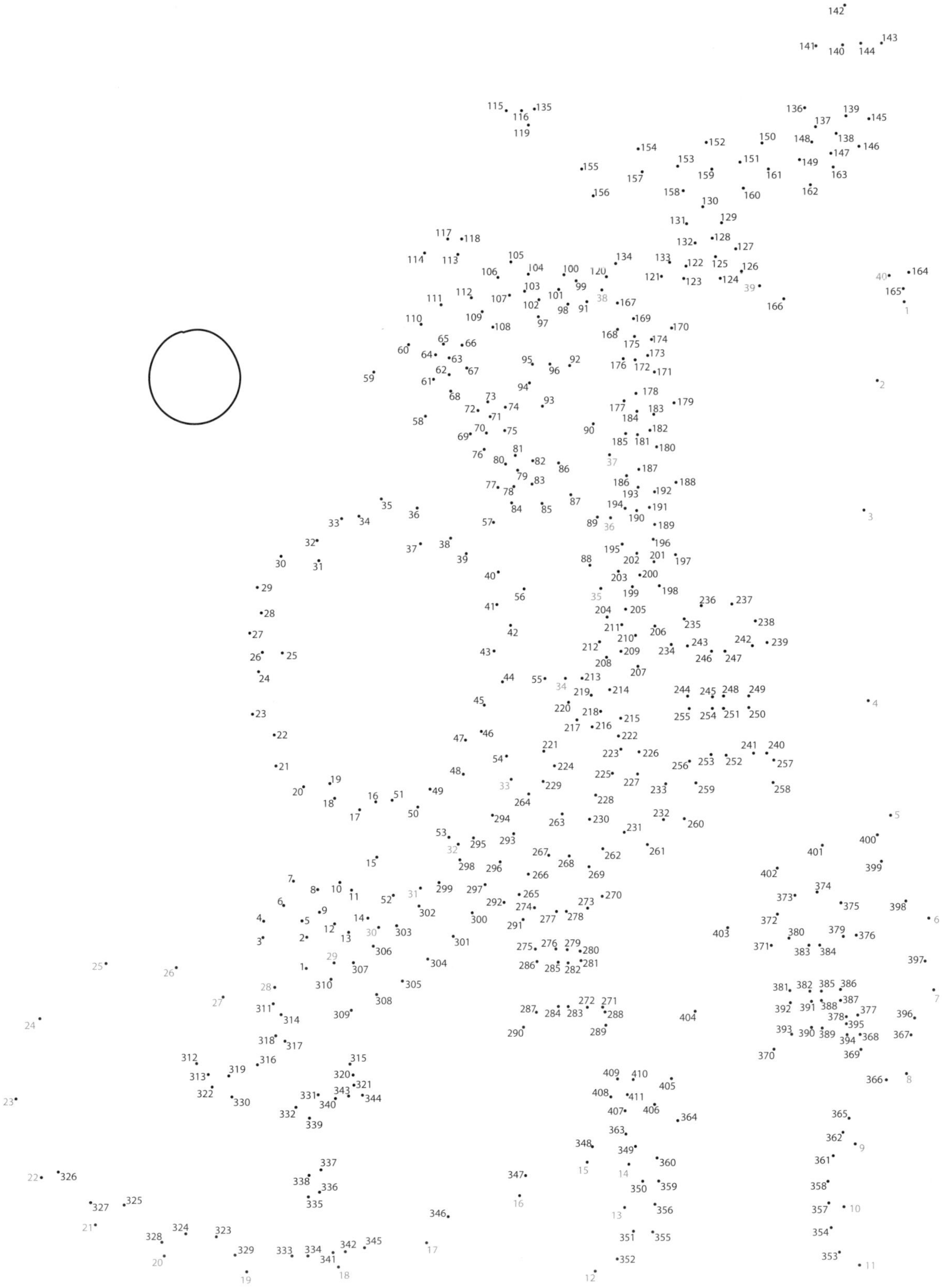

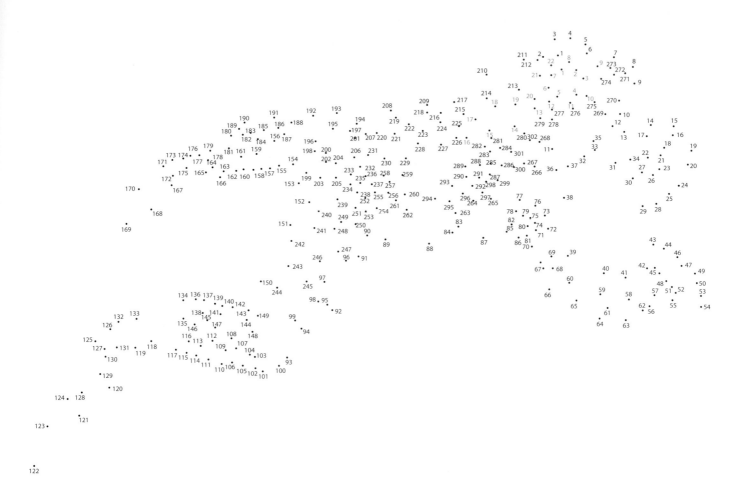

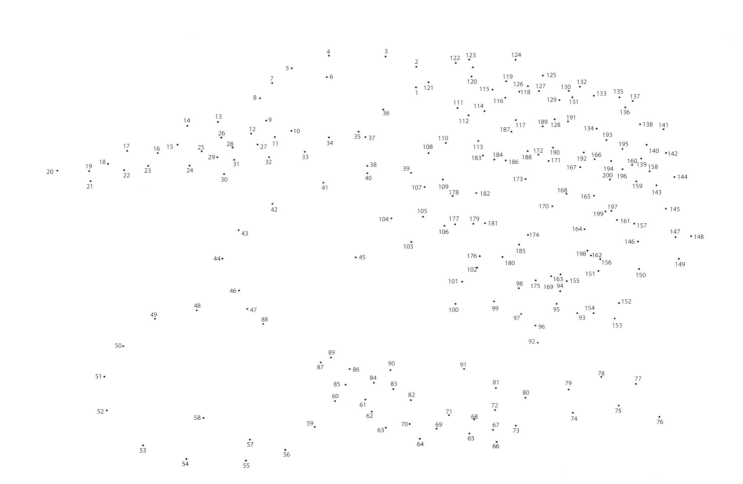

Solutions

page 4

page 5

page 6

page 7

pages 12-13

page 14

page 15

pages 28-29

page 30

page 31

pages 32-33

page 34

page 35

pages 44-45

page 46

page 47

pages 56-57

page 58

page 59

pages 64-65

page 66

page 67

pages 68-69

page 70

page 71

pages 72-73

page 74

page 75

Discover more creativity books,
now available from Studio Press!

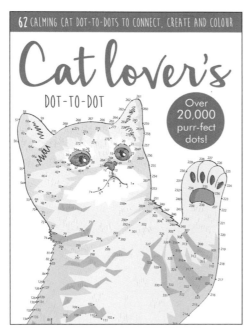

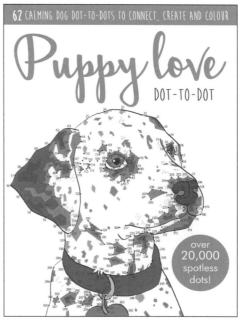

Share with us!